WONDER VERSE

Dreams On Paper

Edited By Roseanna Caswell

First published in Great Britain in 2025 by:

Young Writers
Remus House
Coltsfoot Drive
Peterborough
PE2 9BF
Telephone: 01733 890066
Website: www.youngwriters.co.uk

Book Design by Davina Hopping

Softback ISBN 978-1-83685-066-3
Printed and bound in the UK by BookPrintingUK
Website: www.bookprintinguk.com
YB0621D

FOREWORD

Welcome Reader,

For Young Writers' latest competition *Wonderverse*, we asked primary school pupils to explore their creativity and write a poem on any topic that inspired them. They rose to the challenge magnificently with some going even further and writing stories too! The result is this fantastic collection of writing in a variety of styles.

Here at Young Writers our aim is to encourage creativity in children and to inspire a love of the written word, so it's great to get such an amazing response, with some absolutely fantastic pieces. This open theme of this competition allowed them to write freely about something they are interested in, which we know helps to engage kids and get them writing. Within these pages you'll find a variety of topics, from hopes, fears and dreams, to favourite things and worlds of imagination. The result is a collection of brilliant writing that showcases the creativity and writing ability of the next generation.

I'd like to congratulate all the young writers in this anthology, I hope this inspires them to continue with their creative writing.

CONTENTS

THE
CREATIVE
WRITING

The Enchanted Secret

In a forest where whispers dance with the breeze,
Lived a girl named Elara, among the tall trees.
With a secret so bright, she could speak to the birds,
And make flowers bloom with the softest of words.

One sunny morning, she wandered away,
And found a small fox, lost, in dismay.
"Dear Finn," she said, with a heart full of care,
"Don't worry, sweet friend, we'll find your home there."

Through emerald trees, hand in paw they did roam,
Meeting wise owls and rabbits, all far from their home.
Each creature they met shared stories of cheer,
Filling Elara's heart with joy and with fear.

As sunset painted the sky warm and gold,
They found Finn's family, their love shining bold.
"Thank you, dear friend, for believing in me!"
Finn's eyes sparkled bright, like the stars by the sea.

With a smile, Elara embraced her own light,
Her magic was meant to bring joy, pure and bright.
From that day forth, with the forest she'd share,
Her enchanted spirit, a love everywhere.

Khalid Suluub (10)

Autumn

Amber leaves fall from the trees,
Whispering winds dance with ease.
Crisp crackles sound beneath my feet,
As nature's colours are so sweet.

Beneath the branches, red and gold,
Rustling leaves that never get old.
A gentle breeze brings giggles and fun,
Autumn's magic has just begun!

Pumpkins sit in patches so bright,
Thump! They fall in the soft twilight.
Harvest moons glowing like a lamp,
Fields all dressed in a cosy stamp.

Cider scents and spices fill the air,
Every sip makes me stop and stare.
Nature wraps us in a warm hug,
While cuddly blankets make us snug.

As dusk falls, a soft whoosh goes,
Owls in trees, as nighttime glows.
They hoot and watch from high above,
While we share stories, laughter, and love.

Chilly nights and stars up high,
Crickets sing their lullaby.
Under the moon, bright and round,
Magic and wonder can always be found.

Campfires crackle, flames dance around,
Marshmallows toast with a sweet, soft sound.
We tell spooky tales and laugh so loud,
Autumn nights make us feel so proud.

As frost starts to cover the ground,
Webs sparkle like jewels all around.
The world changes, but it's still so neat,
In autumn's charm, life feels complete.

So let's explore these colourful days,
Hold onto the magic in so many ways.
For autumn's gifts are treasures to find,
In every leaf, a story combined!

Rahi Vaghasia (10)

Fireflies

Have you ever seen a firefly?
I bet not, don't lie.
The way they fly, and flutter and glow,
Will surely have your minds blown.
Fly, little fireflies, fly!
As they float dreamily, into the night sky.

They live in swarms, floating around,
Until a great big owl, who has them found.
Oh no! Oh no! That's no good!
You don't want to be slurped up like soup!
Fly, little fireflies, fly!
As they float dreamily, into the night sky.

As you might have known,
The fireflies' tails have always glowed.
Lighting their merry way,
Driving the darkness away.
Fly, little fireflies, fly!
As they float dreamily, into the night sky.

Over the centuries, they haven't much evolved,
As slowly the things around them begin to resolve.
It is very clear that in the long ago,
The fabulous fireflies still had their glorious glow

Fly, little fireflies, fly!
As they float dreamily, into the night sky.

Now let's all see the yummy things they eat.
They have worms, snails, slugs, and some tasty nectar treats!
And even though their lives are only sixty-one days,
They have enough time to eat and play.
Fly, little fireflies, fly!
As they float dreamily, into the night sky.

Fly, little fireflies, fly!
Fly, little fireflies, fly!
Fly, little fireflies, fly!
As they float dreamily, into the night sky.

Leo Cheung (10)

Clickety Clack

My eyes darted open.
Clickety-clack
A voice struck out in the internal darkness of the
decaying carriage.
Clickety-clack
Calling me forward.
Clickety-clack
I lurched, lumbered and limped towards the blood-
curdling voice as it pierced through the silence.
Clickety-clack
"Where am I, and why am I here?"
Clickety-clack
The odious smell and dampness and decay crept
up my nose.
Clickety-clack
The menacing and cunning cackle of the mysterious
voice was too deafening to ignore.
Clickety-clack
The spiteful voice finally spoke up
Clickety-clack
"Why are you here?"
Clickety-clack
"I'll tell you why you are here."
Clickety-clack

The malevolent ice-blue eyes flashed through the dust.
Clickety-clack
The light flicked off
Clickety-clack
I was shrouded in darkness.
Clickety-clack
The lighting roared and screeched.
Clickety-clack
I squinted, though I wish I didn't.
Clickety-clack
I fell to the floor
Clickety-clack
The train around me disappeared
Clickety-clack
Everything faded
Clickety-clack
"Nooo!"
Clickety-clack
The last thing I heard was this:
Clickety-clack.

Livinia Ganatra (9)

Sad Little Cloud

In the sky so vast and true,
A little cloud wandered, feeling quite blue
Its edges dropped, and its fluff was thin
And it pondered why it could not grin
"Dear Cloud," said the sun with care
"Why do you wear that miserable air?
The cloud sighed gently, raindrops near
"I'm just a little bit sad, I fear
You see he went on,
I miss my friends who danced and bend
They've twirled and twisted out of sight
And now I miss them day and night"
The sun smiled softly its rays shining bright
"Loneliness is like a starless night
But look around, my friend, there's even joy
When hearts mend, for example
A rainbow after rain
Colours blending, happiness regained
And when the night turns dark
And stars shimmer
Secrets they keep"
The cloud listened, his hope starting to sprout
Maybe sadness was not eternal misery

With every minute ticking away
Sadness could be a misunderstood feeling
So it floated as high as possible
And embraced the cool breeze
Whispering to the flowers and the trees
So as the sun drifted below the hill
The cloud found reassurance, a newfound thrill
So he discovered even in sadness, there's a happy ending
Room for growth for stars aligning
So our little cloud started to smile
Knowing sadness was only for a little while.

Leah Germain (10)

Talentless Teenagers

Someone once asked me
"What do you want to be when you grow up?"
It was a simple answer, really
Not everyone had a mind
Of wondrous imagination
To even picture what
They were going to be when they grew up
I didn't crave the world's embrace
I didn't want to be in the limelight
I didn't want to seek glory in grand peaks
Just the comfort of quiet nights.
I didn't want to be an astronaut
I didn't want to be the world's best chef
I didn't want to be a miracle doctor
I didn't want to be a life-changing lawyer
I didn't want to be a skilled actor or a swimmer
I didn't want to excel in sports or academics
I didn't have the motivation to own a business
I lacked the determination for ideas
To become an engineer
The thought of becoming a teacher made
Me sick to the bone.
And why would I want to be an explorer?

Searching the depths of the sea
Or the mysteries of a mountain
Such pointless decisions
I didn't want to be everything divine
Just a breath in the wind
A grain of sand
A note in a chord
Dissolving into the whole
Forever unheard
No dreams
No success
I didn't want to be
Destined greatness,
Just nothing
And nothing different.

Inaya Ngoy (11)

A Turtle's Journey

The moon shone bright
On the sandy beach
A turtle washed up on the shore
The sea just out of reach

Laden with eggs
She carried her kin
Counting on fate
To not do them in

With a heavy heart
She abandoned her spawn
Reaching the sea
At the break of dawn

The eggs went *crack*
As the hatchlings crept out
They were all nervous
Without a doubt

One of the group
Fell behind the rest
As the hatchling readied
For the ultimate test

A voice inside him
Urged him into the sea
Questioning his existence
And yearning to be free

The salty sea air
Brought tears to his eyes
Beyond the waves
Was the ultimate prize

Forwards he trudged
But found himself tangled
In the grip of a net
That could get him strangled

His flailing limbs
Caused the net to fray
Releasing him from the trap
That held him in its sway

The cry of a gull
Made him jump with alarm
But his speedy reactions
Saved him from harm

After escaping
From creatures so vile

The little hatchling
Allowed himself a smile

With a final heave
And a tremendous splash
The turtle entered the sea
And was gone in a flash.

Rishi Ramprakash (10)

Wonderverse

M orning cracked in the sky,
A nd the sun shone its rays down,
G ood morning Szajiny, Srisha and Janu!
I t's a lovely day, isn't it girls?
C ome on, let's play a game

A n aroma of spices flew from the kitchen to my nose,
N ow that's how I can tell if it's time for breakfast or not
D ashing through the kitchen, we followed Mother.

W arm foods were prepared on the long mahogany table.
A s always, Srisha, Janu, and Father waited for me.
R ibbons of red were on our chairs and I ate my delicious dish absorbing the taste of curries.
M other really cooks the best!
T ime for a game of chess!
H eading with a hearty meal, we started our game.

S haring stories while playing,
P raising each other,
A nd testing
R inging with race,
K icking off a game was always the key.

Szajiny Srikanth (12)

A Secret, Magic Book Of Grandma's

In the attic's dust twilight, the found tomb,
Its cover was worn and ancient, like a whisper from a distant home.
With trembling hands, they opened wide the book of Grandma's lore,
And suddenly, they tumbled through a magic, hidden door.

Their world became a pastoral landscape, with colours bright and bold,
The air was sweet like honey, and the ground was paved with gold.
Trees whispered secrets, rivers sang with crystal notes,
An adventure lay before them, one to overcome.

Through enchanted forests, and skies of twilight blue,
They met creatures of legend and dangers they never knew.
Each step was like a heartbeat, pounding with delight,
For in this fairytale land, their spirits too took flight.

Alas, they reached the castle, with turrets to the sky,
Its walls were made of cosmic dust, and the gates were open wide.

Inside, upon a throne, with a crown with silver glimmer,
Sat Grandma, wise and regal, like a vision from
a dream.

Her eyes sparkled with stories, her smile a guiding light,
For she was the ruler of this land, in the endless night.
Their hearts swelled with wonder, and pride began
to bloom,
Knowing Grandma's fairytale was their family's
hidden secret.

Tanvi Kuncham (10)

My Piece Of Jannah

Emeralds as green as grass,
Rubies as red as red velvet roses,
Sapphires that shine
As bright as the deep blue sea.

Aromatic plants and flowers
That bloom in every shade of colour.
Shiny pearls that illuminate
Your pathway to heaven's gate.
All the birds of Jannah
Sit down to sing you a melodious tune.
The golden smile of the sun so bright
Fills your heart with happiness and delight.

As quick as a lightning flash,
Beautiful sweet-smelling flowers appear
in front of you,
Welcoming you with dazzling colours.
All the magnificent prophets
(May Allah's peace and blessing be upon them)
Line up to meet you with the greetings of Salam.

The juicy mouth-watering exotic fruits
Make your stomach rumble with delight.
As soon as you think of something to eat

It magically appears in front of your eyes.
As soon as you think of the gushing chocolate fountain,
A tranquil chocolate river flows beside you
Making you jump out of joy.

As soon as you lay down,
Perfect pillows form and feel as soft as clouds.

All the miraculous planets, human beings
And animals bow down to the
One True Lord,
The Lord of Majesty and Grace.

Bilal Mangera (8)

The Maze Of Maths

Oh gosh, those numbers that dance in endless rows,
Equations that twist like a tangled hose
With fractions fighting for their place,
I'm lost in the symbols, with a perplexed face.

Why must you taunt me, my dearest maths?
With your theorems and your strangling wrath?
Graphs that curve and angles that bend,
Each problem is like a labyrinth with no end.

You whisper to me consistently, quite sweetly, "Just solve for x,"
Yet here I am, feeling quite vexed.
Pi never ends, it mocks me and I'm in fright
Infinite digits, for me a restless night

And who came up with prime and composite?
A code so complex, a cryptic maze
Oh great! Statistics, with your mean and your mode,
Why must you make me carry such a heavy load?

Algebra and geometry too, each chapter is a challenge,
Each theorem has a whole different clue.
I plead for some peace, just a moment's relief
From the chaos of numbers, I can hardly believe.

Yet deep down I know, that amidst all the stress,
You shape our so-called world, you breathe in life, you are life!
So I'll grumble and moan, but I'll stay forever with you
For in your never-ending maze, I manage to find my way.

Amaarah Hussain (12)

A Sloth's World

See me hanging from a tree
That is where I'm meant to be
Sleeping all day and night
I'll be lucky if I see the light
Some say I'm lazy, some say I'm cute
Others say sloths are just dirty brutes
Two-toed or three-toed
We eat so much we might explode
Scruffy or neat
Kids still think I'm extremely sweet
In scorching sun or heavy rain
We stay suspended all the same
We always win at hide-and-seek
To stay away from harpy eagles' beaks
When a hungry jaguar comes to prey
Our algae-covered fur gives nothing away
Through a healthy diet of leaves and fruit
The rainforest provides us with lots of food
We are in no rush to eat it all
If you want to join us, just give us a call
We have been around since dinosaur times
Us sloths may be slow, but we are steady and fine
Don't cut the tropical forest

That's our home
It's our protective dome
It has given us food, shelter and space
At this rate of the tree-cutting race
We will all be homeless and displaced
In a fast-moving world
Our slow-paced life is Olympic gold
Learn from us to take time to rest
And protect the forests as they are the best.

Tessa Dijkstra (8)

Magic

Whispers in the night, stars dancing in the silver sky,
As dreams take flight in the moonlight,
Slowly the shadows join the dance
On moonlit paths, we tread with every step,
A secret spell we sow, where dreams take flight,
And fears can rest instead. The flicker of a wand,
A playful spark, with bright laughter, we chase
the dark.

The magic of life intertwined with the moments of
our lives.
Though time may fade and seasons change their song,
This spark of wonder lingers in our hearts.
In simple things, we find what keeps us strong,
As magic weaves through life in quiet parts.

Let joy be found in every little thing,
For in each heart, a hidden spell is cast.
Tiny sparks of dreams breaking through the dark,
Making worry disappear like a breath of fresh air,
Leaving behind thoughts of wonder
And the thrill of the unknown.

Laughter spills, as shadows twist and turn,
Each moment is like a trick, a chance to believe,

That the world can be more, just for a heartbeat,
Just for a wish. Magic lives, in our laughter,
In the stories that we tell, a spark in the ordinary,
Waiting to be found.

Lucy Jane (17)

A Destroyed World

Distraught, my once joyful world
Had been polluted and destroyed
It had been the 206th day
That I was trapped in this old dusty hole
And it felt like my entire life was gone
And there was no hope left to find.
I had heard banging all night
And I didn't know what it was.
Upon awakening the next morning
Something cold and grim touched my skin,
It was a gust of wind but how could that be?
Was I free?
There was a faint glimmer of light.
But when I started to explore the new world,
I was not expecting what I was about to see.
Demolished. Wrecked. Ruined.
The sky that I had remembered,
So blue and bright,
Was now hanging heavy clouds.
A horrid stench filled the air
I took a step forward,
My eyes pierced.
I had now spotted abandoned broken cars,

Bent and rust surrounded it
With moss growing underneath
Windows were cracked leaving jagged holes,
Where innocent people used to live.
The sun was blocked out,
The air was filled with melancholy and sorrow,
Not even a breath of hope was alive.
Cold icy sharp fingers grabbed me
Was this the end...?

Anaiah Akinnayajo (12)

Pigs In Wings

Once upon a daisy,
I found a flying pig called Maisie,
She was a little bit crazy,
With a tad of lazy,
She had a friend called Stacy.

These two pigs flew high and low,
Wearing multicoloured bows,
They said they were from a wonderverse,
This made me kind of nervous.
I said, "Why are you here?"
They replied, "To make things clear"
I tilted my head with confusion,
Is this all an illusion?
They snorted in my face
Then vanished without a trace.

I looked around to see where they had gone
They were sitting in a puddle on my lawn.
They made weird sounds,
Wearing funny crowns.
Saying we are going to take over the town
And make it all brown.

I said, "Oh no, you can't
I am going to buy a pig-eating plant."

Maisie and Stacy looked at each other
Both thinking of their mother
They took one look at me
And decided to let me be.
They flew off into the distance
With an electrical resistance.
I watched them fly away
Now I am ready for a new day.

Lilly Tyler (10)

Wonderverse, Where Everything Has A Feeling

I sit on the turf, minding my way,
Gathering sunshine, for rain I pray.
Summer waves goodbye, the leaves darken,
The choir of birdsong, to which I harken.

Then comes October, with whispers of fright
I feel what's coming, the dreaded night.
All through the month, the fireworks explode,
Let them have their fun, I suppose.

A hand reaches down, a sharp knife in its grip,
I shiver inside as they start to snip.
My orange skin, once smooth and round,
Now sliced and diced, for a mere pound.

They scoop out my insides, bit by bit,
Leaving me hollow, barren, unfit.
I feel rotten like half of me has died,
Then all of a sudden, a light burns inside.

My jagged grin, my crooked glare,
A face so terrifying, you couldn't bear.

A friendly soul turned eerie and ghoulish,
To have my old life back is my only wish.

Here I stand on Halloween Eve,
Fulfilling the dreams that children believe,
I'm a tiny piece of this eventful night
Burning happily, like dynamite.

Haydn Wan (8)

My Magical World

Up on the hill, stands a castle
In the sky, are shooting stars
In the meadows, is a bunch of dandelions

Up on another hill, stands a dungeon
In that sky, are falling bombs
In the graveyard, are a bunch of gravestones

Both of these lands are separated by a line
That particular line is forbidden to cross
That's what keeps both sides apart

In the morning, one side is shining
In the morning, one side is enjoying
In the morning, one side is dark
And in the morning, one side is dying

Both of these lands are separated by a line
That particular line is forbidden to cross
That's what keeps both sides apart

One land is magical, one land is not
One land is the best land, one land is not
But both lands combined are the real world
A world of equality, a world of truth
A world that is magical, a world that is new

A world with inequality, a world of lies
A world that is normcl, a world that is old
But this all makes my magical world.

Kristen Omeata (13)

Popping Pegasus And Fairies

I was running down the road
Because I was late for school,
And I was late to take my tool,
I rushed here, there and everywhere,
But I didn't really take care.
I slipped on a banana peel ready to fall,
Even though I was strong enough to stand up tall.
I closed my eyes in fear and fright,
They both shut down really tight.
But I didn't fall or hurt myself,
Because coming to my aid was a little elf.
He made me a fairy and gave me his unicorn,
He told me he was recently born,
That made me feel so much better,
That I wrote him a beautiful letter.
The letter had lots of stamps and stickers,
One with his unicorn and a cat called Whiskers,
And another with a cute fairy,
Who really didn't like to be scary,
That made him feel so swift.
So, he made me a pair of kitty ears as a gift,
And a Pegasus called Rainbow Dash,

Because she can move as quickly as a flash.
So that is the story of me and my elf,
And it's time to say goodbye to you.

Hareem Shaikh (7)

Picture Day!

My dad woke me up.
"Nicole, time for school!" he said.
Then I said, "Oh my! It's picture day
I really need to wake up
Because my crush will be next to me!"
Lip gloss - check, hair - check, makeup - check!
I think today I will confess to him.
But the problem is I haven't told any of my friends.
But focus, you need to go to school or you'll be late.
Oh, my days!
My worst enemy, Rebecca, was next to him, Daniel.
And I know why because she also has a crush on him.
So back to what I was saying
We had our picture and mine was horrible
And as if my day couldn't get worse... my dog died.
I was so sad, but Daniel asked if I was okay
Then I started to cry and Daniel hugged me
Aww, that was sweet.
Then he leaned and gave me a kiss
It was so magical
Until I heard someone say,
"Wake up! Wake up!"

"What!"
My mom said, "Wake up, you're late!"
No! It was all a dream!

Nicole Fortes Dias (10)

Heart Of Game

In fields of green and courts of gold.
My heart beats fast, leading the way.
From sunrise runs to evening drills.
In every sport, my spirit thrills.

The echo of a ball's sharp crack.
A final sprint, no turning back.
The crowd's roar, a silent prayer.
Each moment was played with utmost care.

Through sweat and tears, through joy and pain.
In victory's light or loss' rain,
I find myself, in every stride.
My passion burning deep inside.

For in these games, I feel alive.
The thrill of pushing to survive.
With every race, with every score,
I crave the challenge, wanting more.

The team, the bond, the shared embrace.
The lessons learned in every race.
In sports, I find a place to grow.
A love that only athletes know.

So here I stand, with dreams untold.
With stories written, brave and bold.
For in my love of sport, I see.
The best of life, the best of me.

Pareeza Umar (12)

The Flight Of The Unicorn

Here alone in the night, I walked,
Who knew what I would find,
Trekking through the forest, however,
A sudden mist descended.

I couldn't find my way around,
As an unexpected glow alit.
I couldn't believe my eyes,
As a majestic creature approached.

A pair of glossy white wings were folded to its side,
With a gleaming golden horn,
It stared at me with brilliant blue eyes,
As its tail swished around.

It bowed its head in my direction,
And I stood transfixed.
It was a beautiful unicorn,
It trotted to me.

Soon it was beside me,
And its eyes travelled to mine.
It looked like it wanted me to grab hold,
So I clambered onto its back.

With a smooth motion, it took off,
Soaring through the sky.
I could see little houses zooming past,
Like tiny glowing dots.

However, the amazing journey came to an end,
And I saw my familiar house,
As I slid off its silky back, it purred gently,
It touched its horn to me and took off into the night sky.

Kristen Lee (10)

Mad Hatter

Falling through the rabbit hole,
It feels like I lost my soul,
Finally, we reach the sand,
To the one and only Wonderland,
Seeing mushrooms as tall as me,
Then comes a rabbit you see,
Checking if he's on time,
To see if he fits in this rhyme,
Bright colours it's like a dream,
Here comes a man walking on a beam,
Red rivers filled with treats,
A tea party with filled seats,
I come to sit down,
They are happy, not a single frown,
He asked, "Some tea?"
"Yes!" I drank with glee,
Mad Hatter was his name,
He was known for his fame,
He was old and turned mad,
Which made his daughter sad,
Sadly, I had to make my way,
"Goodbye!" they would say,
I looked everywhere,

Until I saw the very same hare,
"Where do I go now?" I said,
The hare kept shaking his head,
He whimpered, "You can't leave,"
I went on to grieve,
I stayed there for many years,
Small doors, twisted trees
And talking to my peers,
I will plan my escape,
One day.

Sara Bulina (10)

First Day At My New School

Emerging out of my soft bed and coming down
the stairs.
Somehow, I forget it is today that I must face my fears.

As I walk in, and through the gates, with butterflies in
my tummy,
My knees tremble, my palms sweat, and I start to miss
my mummy.

Children laughing, skipping, jumping altogether now,
Cartwheeling gymnasts, staring eyes, I will make
friends somehow.

Lining up and walking in, with people pushing past,
Teacher's footsteps, a friendly face, I sit at the back
of class.

Learning and listening, sitting still, sorting all the cards.
Playtime comes and I eat my snack. Meeting friends
is hard.

Later on, a scrumptious lunch to balance on
colourful trays.
Back to class and in our seats, we learn in an
exciting way.

A loud bell rings, they call my name, and the day is nearly done.
I grab my coat, I feel so proud, it's all been so much fun.

Imogen Newman (7)

Imagination

I magine, a world free of harm, free of enslavement, free of hunger, free of poverty, free of war, free of life's lies.
M aybe our world, an abundant, carefree world; it would be like waking to a dream, wouldn't it? Well, that is our choice to make.
A charming place, hidden within the universe.
G reeting each other with a pleasant smile.
I had a dream just like that one. I still do.
N ow, we don't need to do a whole lot of work to make everyone happy,
A lthough we may do as we like.
T oday or tomorrow, I want everyone to smile, a real smile.
I love it when people smile. A small smile, a big smile, who cares?
O n this planet, together we can make a change. We can do whatever. But we all must contribute. Don't ruin our divine home.
N ot one, but all people, can live together in peace.

That is my dream.

Jasmine Koc

Counting

C ounting, whether it's counting stars, counting people or counting on your loved ones, waiting, to make something right. Make sure it's right
O ne, two, three and four. I count the seconds as they flee, ticking countless moments lost to me
U p, up and up. I watch leaves flying high. How high do they go till they reach the sky?
N umbers I count, one, two, three, how many fail till I make one successfully
T ens and thousands of stars, I count in the sky at night, how many more hours till I see the daylight?
I nventing a time machine would be a whole lot of fun, counting back the years to when I was one
N ever forget your loved ones count, the love inside couldn't be such a big amount
G rateful, remember to be grateful every single day because you never know when your life will turn grey.

Elliott Jones (11)

Pink

I used to think pink was my colour
I used to think I looked beautiful in pink
Until one day it was different
I was growing older and wiser
And pink felt weird
It felt like I needed to be more mature
And stick with natural colours like black.
I grew more mature and wore black for one day
I felt more wise and independent
And like I was going to fit in,
Until I saw a girl wearing pink
She looked pretty and beautiful
Like it was her colour
Like she had to never grow out of pink, like me
She didn't look childish
She looked like any other student,
Perfectly fit in.
That's when I realised
I didn't have to give up pink
It could have been my colour
I didn't have to give it up at all

Just because I'm growing up
Doesn't mean I should throw away what I love
So from then on, I wore pink and still fit in.

Leila-Rose Williams (10)

Spring-Love Coming

Spring is coming tonight with magic around.
The hope of light is coming with love.
And never let go.

Flowers grow in spring.
So does my love for you.

Love stays in a box full of memories and never escapes.
It is like a cave that no one has ever seen.

A pot of gold is better than a diamond.
Never would you meet a monster.
That is never too late to be a friend.

Somebody knocked at my door.
Slowly I opened it but nobody was there.
Or was someone hiding behind my door
Shadows in my mind.

When I opened my door there was mindful music
Coming through my ears.
I felt like I was diving into a pool of music flying around me
I felt powerful like diamonds blooming like a shooting star.

There were a lot of musical instruments.
There was a piano called 'pelifement'
Because it was gloomy like life.

Sofia Maragkoudaki (7)

Celestial Wonders

In the vast expanse of night,
Stars ignite with ancient light,
Galaxies in endless dance,
A cosmic waltz, a timeless trance.

Nebulas in colours bright,
Paint the sky with sheer delight,
Planets spin in silent grace,
Each one holds a secret place.

Comets blaze with fiery tails,
Whispering their cosmic tales,
Black holes lurk with hidden might,
Swallowing the endless night.

Constellations weave their lore,
Stories from the days of yore,
Orion's belt, the Pleiades,
Guardians of celestial seas.

In this wonderverse so grand,
Mysteries lie close at hand,
From the smallest atom's spin,
To the universe's grand design.

We gaze in awe, our hearts alight,
With dreams of stars and endless night,
For in this vast, eternal sea,
We find our place, our destiny.

Rabia Dar (12)

The Oooooflagmatutu

Inhumanly tall, the size of a mountain
Fingers like forks and feet like skewers on the barbie.
The oooooflagmatutu, 'tis a vegan monster
Who lives on a diet of curtains
And loves to drink seawater.
Buoyant it is, with an inflatable bum,
And loves a splendiferous day of fun.
It lives in a mound of metal,
And sleeps on a water bed of rum.
Thieves would stare in wonder
At this creature's ability to steal noses from
right under!
It has spikes on its body you say... what for?
You may wonder...
To grate cheese for the mice he meets every Tuesday...
of course!
As we come to the end of the oooooflagmatutu story,
We learn one final thing,
You will never meet another creature as interesting,
If you wish to meet him again... just wait till
next spring!

Demir Sahbaz (10)

The Magical Doors

As you go through the magical doors,
You can experience the wonderland.
With cotton candy clouds and silver floors,
And beaches with golden magical sand.

Go farther and see fantastic creatures,
Big and small with different patterns.
You will be lucky to have no teachers,
And before your eyes, the world turns.

The sky was filled with bright lightning,
You feel an icy shiver down your spine.
Monsters stalk the land; it is frightening,
It's most divine, that you want to report crime.

So you run and scream away from the beasts,
You are very glad to be back at home.
You feel a tingly feeling in your feet,
You know the monsters are still out to roam.

You want to go back to the wonderland,
But it is too scary, you understand.

Ella Koc (9)

Nightmare Or Dream?

I'm sleeping soundly in my bed,
But things carry on in my head.
I'm screaming or dreaming in my sleep.
I dream I'm on a marshmallow cloud.
It is not loud.
There are other clouds above me,
They do not love me.
They throw things (not at my head.)

Is this a dream or a nightmare?
In the morning I won't care.
I do now.
Why couldn't I have a dream with a cow?
I go to sleep the next night I'm led in my bed.
I'm riding on a dragon.
They like eating salmon and are wet.

I want this dream to last forever,
To end never.
I wake up.
I go to sleep and embrace the dream,
It's of a world that's totally clean.
Tomorrow I'll do my best for the planet.
Not in my bed, not in my head.

Grace Cook (10)

The Horn

As I wandered through the weary, worn woods,
I saw something I thought my eyes would never see.
A mystical, mighty beast staring right at me,
It all looked strong and powerful.
It was built like a beautiful machine.
Yet it seemed in pain,
It was yelping and limping.
Who was dumb enough to save this creature...
Me of course!
As I lurched forward,
I had to remain calm.
I looked at its leg and it seemed to have...
A horn stuck in it.
I held on tight,
I held on tighter,
I held on with my very tightest and raised it out.
It bowed down and offered me to keep the horn,
I was very amazed at this as you would expect.
As I wandered through the weary, worn woods,
I saw something I thought my eyes would never see.

Maya Pugh (11)

My True Best Friend

Terrific tulips shining bright,
Wonderful blue tits in the light.
Nothing feels hollow when you are with me,
Everything seems fun as far as I can see.
Beautiful butterflies as blue as the sea,
You are the key to my destiny.
Lovely leaves on tremendous trees,
I really love those buzzy bees.
You are like a rose, it's so true,
That is why I chose you.
You are my best friend who is always there,
To laugh and cry, to show you care.
You are my guiding light
Through the darkness of the night.
You are my friend who is always near
To chase away my every fear.
You are a shining star
Whose love and light will take me far.
You are a precious gift every day,
You hold onto me if I float away.
You are my true best friend
Forever and ever till the end!

Anna Abbott (9)

The Wizard

A hundred years ago,
In a land far from here,
The wizard slowly staggers.
Autumnal leaves crunch underfoot,
As he breathes the misty air, like a dragon of old.
Enveloped by the lush, green forest
That carefully hides his precious secrets.

His face, gentle and caring
Frames his glittering emerald eyes,
That promises magic and adventure.
A glossy, pearl-white beard dangles,
Like fishing bait on his shiny blue rod.

Down by the sparkling river,
He glances at the weathered, birch door.
Creaking ajar, his humble cottage welcomes him.
Inside this peaceful place, he creates.

His dutiful cauldron, filled to the brim, bubbles.
His is beyond time, beyond this world.
A rule breaker,
A potion maker
A spell caster
Brewing faster.

Jackson Hill (10)

The Great Fire Of London

On 2nd September on Pudding Lane,
A fire started and caused great pain!

Early one night when it was dark,
An oven was still burning and out jumped a spark!

The fire was starting to spread!
When everyone was still in bed.

They all woke up the mayor when he was still in bed.
When he was dreaming about bread.

They were all scared and frightened
There was no emotion for delighted

They woke up the King who widened with shock!
Then he shouted, "We need a fire hock!"

They threw lots and lots of water
The fire and flames were a great big causer!

It burned down streets
And all the meat

Which all felt sad
But others were mad!

Aylin Jappens (7)

Black And White

In shades of black, the night is deep,
Where silent stars in stillness sleep.
A cloak of mystery draped in the air,
Hiding truths we do not dare.

In white, the morning softly wakes,
With quiet light that gently breaks.
It tells of hope, a canvas bare,
Of dreams and paths that lead somewhere.

Black is the unknown, vast and wide,
A whispered fear we cannot hide.
White is the calm, the peaceful grace,
That brings us warmth in its embrace.

Together they dance, the light, the dark,
A perfect balance, a vivid spark.
For in their union, truth is found,
In every shadow, in every sound.

Black and white, the contrasts blend,
A timeless story with no end.

Bridget Frimpong (17)

The Pixie

Bewitching the mind and the senses
Inspiring joy, fluttering with liveliness
It wasn't the mighty god
But a seemingly insignificant pixie

Its shimmering wings weaved in and out of the grass
The gleam in its eye twinkling with mischief
Its laugh is so peculiar yet so enchanting
This tiny sprite was a dangerous wonder

In the forest, lush and green
Was a pixie full and free
Stars lit up the night sky
While the sun shone with its intensity

Flowers bloomed ahead, creatures crawled and cried
Clouds like candyfloss, grass like sugar blades
But in the centre was the little pixie, the life for it all
Sometimes the small things are the key to perfection.

Kurtis Chang (12)

Friendship Isn't Just Friends

In the garden of life, friendship blooms like a flower brightening each day
Together, we stand through all the storms of life, stronger as one

In laughter, we find the joy that fills the empty space, hearts light as feathers
Through tears, we remain connected by bonds that last infinitely
And though in silence, we know words are not always needed,
Understanding flows

With each sunrise comes renewed hope for what's in store
As friends we endure
Through thick and thin our friendship will never end
Forever cherished in the dance of life
Friends are our steady partners guiding us with love
So let us rejoice in the gift of true friendship forever cherished.

Hafsah Qasim (9)

Journey

You are off on the journey
Where will you go?
Will you swim underwater?
Or walk in the snow?

Where should we start?
Where should we end?
Will we go climbing?
Should we bring a friend?

Will we go bike riding?
Which bridge should we go through?
Well, are you coming or not?
It's totally up to you!

Jump into a hot air balloon,
Quick, while the fire still shines bright!
Untie the rope on the ground,
Then you're off on your first flight!

First to the candyfloss mountain!
It'll be a wonderful sight!
But let's go there fast,
I bet you'll want to fly my kite!

Oh, look we are nearly there!
So come and be my guest!
Take off your hat and scarf,
And I'll do the rest.

Alexandra Webbe (8)

Friendship

It's magical, it's amazing
It's true, it's strong,
They help you fit in
Friends make you belong!

Sometimes it can splatter
And blow up in your face,
But when you're with your friends
There's no better place!

Friends make things bright and fun
They lift you if you fall,
They're there so you're not lonely
And together you have a ball!

Sometimes friends can argue
Sometimes friends can fall out,
But friendships can't break
And you'll always figure it out!

It's magical, it's amazing
It's true, it's strong,
They help you fit in
Friends make you belong!

Esmé Buttigieg (9)

Winter Forest

I trudged through the dense forest on the path to pain.
The towering trees of overwhelmed confusion
surrounded me.
As I marched on, the moon shone down,
And trees grabbed at me in eerie silence.

As I started cautiously running,
The sorrowful leaves felt like giants above me.
The dense clouds snuck up on me.
Bats soared through the night, as owls hooted.

Twigs snapped from the sharp claws of creatures
hunting.
Leaves crunched as I ran through.
The decaying bark felt rough and jagged as my fingers
swiped it.
Moss rotted and the stench filled the air.
The howling wind whipped my face and sent a shiver
down my spine.

Winter was calling.

Joey Needleman (10)

The Enchanting Castle

Far through the forest,
Way down deep,
A castle stands tall,
Strong and not cheap.

Inside this castle,
It's beautiful and neat,
Everything sparkling, shimmering and clean,
And in the centre of the front room
There's an elegant seat.

It looks as if a princess has lived here,
Maybe even a royal queen,
There are several glass cabinets
Full of glass, plates and china,
It feels like you're on a big movie screen.

It feels enchanting and something from a fairy tale,
Glorious and definitely surreal,
It feels as if you're floating just like a fairy would,
Just like Tinker Bell would or any of her friends.

Poppy-Mae McAuley (10)

The Beach

The waves moved back and forth like a metronome,
As I sat back on my beach chair.
The sand felt like bristles from a comb,
And the breeze felt like skincare.

My sunglasses protected me from the hot, shining sun,
Whilst the kids played with the beach ball and had
lots of fun.
We got in the water and got all wet,
And played some games and placed a bet.

Told my sister to make a castle from sand,
Using a toothpick and only her left hand.
It was quite big, astonishing and wide,
But in the end, it was destroyed by the tide.

That was my day on the beach, it was fun!
Hopefully, I can go back and have another one!

Roisin Mary Cunningham (10)

Dodgeballs In Space

D odging all that comes upon
O bjectives always new
D eviant but round, floating around
G oing away and coming back unexpectedly
E xecrable things can happen
B alls bigger than you think
A ll of the players are aliens
L osers go back home
L oving what they do
S pectators cheering for their team

I t isn't that easy
N iftier as you go

S eeing it is amazing
P opping balloons fill the air
A t the end for late people to see who won
C heering for the winners
E verything might go wrong.

Asana Draman (8)

Creature

C reepy, luminous eyes, void of colour, stared at the city before him.
R esurrected from the mummy's tomb, he stood without patience.
E scaping to terrorise citizens, he was as ferocious as a wild wolf.
A ttempting to take over every city as revenge for how they mistreated him.
T eeth rotting like a haunted soul, bugs crawled out of his mouth as they ran for safety.
U ltimate power bleeding out of his fingers, as his ancestors would have done before him.
R adiant skin beamed into the distance, creating a stairway back to Earth.
E very man, woman and child feared the creature.

Tony Kopa (10)

Scottish Wars Of Independence

Haiku poetry

Independence wars,
They are fighting by the shores,
Just like maniacs.

English fight to win,
It is a terrible sin,
They fight like devils.

Brave Scottish people,
Fighting for Scottish freedom,
Fight Edward's army.

Gentle Margaret dies,
Hear the weeping and the cries,
Sweet as an angel.

Wallace leads the way,
Alongside Andrew Murray,
You can hear the wind.

You can hear them fight,
You can even hear at night,
Hear the leaves crackle.

Thirteen twenty-eight,
You can drop your heavy weight,
Put down your weapons.

Valeria Shaboldina (9)

Friendship

F riend is what you need
R ight next to you if you need them
I love my friends
E verlasting friendship
N ever stop hugging
D ays playing
S top fighting and be friends
H appy days
I love my friends
P laying all day.

F riends all day long
R epeating
I love my friends
E very day playing
N ever break up
D ays are fun with friends
S ummer beach time with my friends
H appy all day long
I will forgive you every time
P lay with me.

Ava Marie Mckoy (10)

I Think Back

I think back to a time,
When we would sing and rhyme,
We would play in the sun,
Our parents would be mad
But we would have fun.

I think back to memories,
When we would fish and catch bees,
And we would go to the beach,
We played in the sand and drew a peach.

I think back to friendships,
Which started from reception,
Then we all grew up, we became closer,
Which made leaving Year 6 a little bit harder.

I think about the summer holidays,
I remember being nervous each day
The practice runs and maps you drew,
Made me think back to how much I love you!

Ella Dyce (11)

Me

I came home from school smiling hard
I had my dinner, packed my bag
I said, "Let's get out of here and into the van
Our adventure starts here
Let's hear you cheer!"
It took a long time to get there
But I was patient all the way

When I got there I needed to stay
In my bedroom there was a bedside table
Desk, mirror and a doodle
The bathroom was so big
It's the greatest place on earth
For my mother's birthday
I'm going to see my family
And have a big party
But I can't stay forever
So let's leave together.

Sylvie May (7)

Keys

Imagine a world, where each key holds a
forgotten story.
Lost in the past, in a stormy, gory, gagging mess.
Just left to die, in a gust of wind, never to be
seen again.
People come to search for their past,
To find answers to questions they dare not ask.
Each key wears a past, like a forgotten mask.

Some keys are broken, dead,
Vines creeping up them some have said.
A glowing gleam, some may seem.
They are all dead on the inside though.
The keys of the past, the stories that did not last.
They have just fallen into the hands of the cold,
winter past.

Philippa Barratt (10)

Friendship

To care for my friend is what I like to do
Make them feel happy and laugh till we're blue
Go to the park and play silly games
Or maybe even go to the mall
When the trends change

Have an ice cream in the summer together
Or go to school or even class
Through autumn and winter
I will be with you
Thick and thin I'll never leave you

Walking on the crunchy fallen leaves
Or through the soft, white snow
Our friendship will last forever
Even when the ends are loose
I will be your friend until the end
And forgive me if I ever lose you.

Alfreda Fragin (11)

But Still There Was No Sound

The trees swayed in the gentle breeze
and the leaves blew around,
The grass danced and the moonlight sang
but still, there was no sound.
The twigs snapped
and the bushes crunched on the moonlit ground,
the grass danced and the moonlight sang
but still, there was no sound.
The water splashed through the night
and the bird perched on the mound,
the grass danced and the moonlight sang
but still, there was no sound.
The sun rose from its resting place
and shone bold and proud,
the grass danced and the moonlight sang
and all the noise was found.

Bowen McDaniel (10)

A Magical Creature...

In a cave deep and dark, I lie in wait
With treasures beside me, a shimmering fate
My scales gleam gold, my wings stretch wide
None dare approach, for many have tried
I breathe out fire, a scorching flame
Those who challenge seldom leave the same
I slumber through ages, yet awake when near
A knight with a sword or a kingdom in fear
Legends are told of the havoc I bring
With claws that are sharp and a tail that can sting
I rule over mountains, I rule over men
Whose stories are told again and again?
What am I?

Answer: A dragon!

Aihem Saber (10)

My Wonder Horse

If I had a pony,
I could call it Tony,
We'd spend every day together,
And be with each other forever,

We would go for a trot,
Walk and jump a lot,
We'd go round and round in canter,
If only I got a pony from Santa,

I wouldn't mind having to muck,
So long as my pony didn't buck,
It would be worth the hours it takes to groom,
To ride through fields of bloom,

And if you couldn't guess,
There are clues in the way I dress,
I'm not just a normal pedestrian,
I'm a born equestrian!

Megan Skitt (9)

The Land Of My Magical Mind

Magical creatures
In this land
Let's go on an adventure
Just take my hand

Just close your eyes
Relax and rest
Then you'll be there
Looking your best

In this world
It has cool features
Like unicorns, dragons
And mythical creatures

Look around
Go and explore
We are not in Chatham
Anymore

Emerald leaves
A sapphire sky

A crystal river
That passes by

When you're ready to leave
This mystical land
All you've got to do
Is take my hand.

Rosie Colley (12)

Magic Waterpark

M agic is the best, power of all.
A magical click and there is a pool.
G igantic slides and fun water rides.
I love the pool,
C ome with me, it'll be cool.

W et and slippery slides,
A s fast as crashing tides.
T oo much fun for all,
E ven children who are small.
R iding waves of magic.
P eople waiting in queues,
A rriving at the waterpark just before noon.
R apidly riding, as fast as lightning.
K indness appears no matter who is near.

Amirah Bekhit (9)

Space Is What You Need!

Look at the stars
Watch the stars
Stare at the stars
The galaxy is waiting for you
Multiple colours are all around you
Look at the planets and enjoy the view
Look at the fun on their faces
And made friendships in the riding spaceship
Let's go everybody, let's go to space
Big, tall, young, small and old, come on
See the sun dancing around
With the moon and other planets liking their view
Aliens and monsters talking and walking on the planets
Oh my gosh, this is amazing
Go to space because space is what you need.

Milena Sowinska (8)

The Animals

The crocodiles have snapping snouts
Which go in every rout

Lions have a thunderous roar
Louder than the tiny boar

The tiger which is fierce and long
Cannot make the loudest roar

The leopard can take over twice its own weight
So you are easy prey if you're eight

The snowy leopard lives in places of snowing
It will hunt you without knowing

The hyena is so strong and cunning
Can eat you with a roar of laughing

And all of them I said so far
Are the ones that like meaty bars.

Sherwin Lucas (10)

My Dream Job

My dream is to be a scientist,
You cure people and diseases,
Work in a lab with chemicals!
So many opportunities,
So many things to discover,
So many role models
Who have uncovered amazing things
Like new periodic elements
And new scientific equations,
I wanna be just like them
And achieve spectacular things,
They are my inspiration and one day
I hope I can make groundbreaking discoveries
Like them and follow in their footsteps,
And not just making the future of science
But being the future of science.

Emmie Jarvis (10)

The Uni-Can Unicorns

Unicorns can be anything or be anyone,
They could be boys or girls,
They could have wings,
They might not,
They would sing,
They would neigh,
They could fly,
They could trot,
They might have friends,
They might be on their own,
They might have ends,
They can live forever,
They can be kind,
They can be mean,
They could like pizza,
They could like beans,
I know one thing for sure,
They're anything you want them to be.
The Uni-can unicorns are extraordinary,
They. Are. Everything.

Nathalia Anais Jackson (9)

The Alien And The Robot

The alien said to the robot
"What does this button do?"
The robot said
"Not to change the subject,
But why are you covered in goo?"

The robot said to the alien
"Why are you so green and tiny?"
The alien said to the robot
"Well, why are you silver and shiny?"

They said,
"Who cares if we're a different race?
It doesn't stop us from sharing space"

Then they talked together for hours and hours
Under the light of the meteor showers.

Jude Hook (7)

Tree Of Energy

Here my friends, today and now
I've got a question to be solved
So raise your hand and shout it out
How many apples can you hold
Before they start to rot and mould
From an apple tree that's tall and green
That gleams at night with fruits and leaves

My friends, I'd also like to know
If you have ever hugged a tree
And have you felt its energy?
I would suggest you doing so
And don't forget to let me know

For now goodbye, I've got to go
But I'll be back with more to know.

Herkus Kuznecovas (9)

The Storm That Came To Pass

Last night it was raining and storming
Mother Nature was warning
Night had struck with lightning
Which was very frightening
Children were crying
As it was oh-so-terrifying
Nightmares had come
While babies suck on their thumb
People didn't know where to run to
What should they do?
The storm started to die down
There was silence throughout the town
There began a brightness
Following a speech from your highness
People began to reappear
There was no more fear
Because summer was here.

Paisley Blu Boslem (9)

The Sneeze

There once was a baboon
Who flew in a balloon
One bright and sunny day
Then down he flew with a big *atchoo!*
That blew all the people away!

There was once a mouse
Who lived in a house
Entirely made of cheese
But then the baboon blew it away
With his one big sneeze!

There was once a pig
Who was fond of wigs,
But then the baboon with his monstrous nose
Blew them away like a powerful hose

Here ends the tale of this monkey
Now tell me, is it really that funky?

Lois Kimnell (10)

The Wild

In the forest the lynx leaps,
Bounding along as silent as the wind on a sunny day.
The lynx stops and starts to creep,
Staring at the deer who trots between the trees of bay.

The lynx leaps and scares the deer,
The lynx slashes, the deer falls dead.
The lynx hears other animals near,
So it eats its fill and bounds home to rest its head.

The other animals fight for the food,
They squark and squabble and be so rude.
A bear roars, the creatures retreat,
This is the wild where animals meet.

Rohan Bull (12)

Letting Go

I stand next to your grave
Tears in my eyes
I look down before looking up at the sky
All I see is darkness without you here

I feel tears on my cheek
I say my last words, "I miss you, my dear"
I just want to say, "I miss having you here"
When you were in my life, you lifted my pain away.

Now that you're gone, all I feel is hurting
Please come back, I feel my life turning
I step back from your grave with one final tear
Before I say, "Goodbye, my dear."

Cleo Lazard-Pearce (11)

Enchanted Escapade

In a huge mess of things, oh my, what a sight!
A toy popped out, a real surprise, alright!
It started chatting, so lively and bright,
Laughs and fun, a magical flight!

It hopped and skipped, a merry old dance,
We ran after it, a wild, joyful prance.
Through the streets, we went in a playful trance,
A grand adventure, full of chance.

Back in its box, the toy did retreat,
The escapade over, a tale so sweet.
Safe and sound, in its cosy seat,
A memory made, a moment to greet!

Adetomi Adeyemi (12)

Wild Weather

Wild winds whistled in the air howling around
Voices echoing getting lost in the wind
Roaring winds powering through the trees.

Blistering hot sun, unbearable heat
Making sweat drive down people's faces
Eye-burning sun blinds you.

Ice-cold rain looks like a mirror
Pouring rain numbing your skin to bone
Freezing rain causes pain.

Puffy clouds a soft ball of rain
Marshmallowy clouds blocking the humid sun
Fog low knee height clouds shallow as can get.

Buddy Cameron (11)

Horses

Horses can canter,
Horses can walk,
Horses can trot,
Horses can do quite a lot.
Their hooves go *clip, clop, clip, clop,*
Horses are gassy sounds like they never stop
They are big and fluffy gentle giants
They are cheeky and can be grumpy
When they trot it can get bumpy
But when they canter
It's as smooth as their big round belly
I do love horses even though
They can sometimes be smelly
When I am with horses, I feel safe and happy.

Liv Kennedy (9)

I Come From

I come from where the sun is hotter than others.
I come from where the weather is colder than other places.
I come from Pakistan, leaving my family.
I come from across the country and sea.
I come from DIY that never got done.
I come from who I trust and I leave, I don't know.
I come from last year and last year how I changed I don't know.
I come to find myself in the mirror and on social media.
I come from where I leave some and now I make some friends.

Salaar Hassan (11)

The Curse Of The Pumpkins

The night was dark,
The thunder crashed,
Below the hill,
Dark waves splashed.
On a hill, there was a graveyard house,
All was silent apart from a mouse.
Four boys carving their pumpkins together,
Not knowing their pumpkins,
Would haunt them forever.
As the moonlight started to rise,
The pumpkins winked their candlelit eyes.
The boys, they screamed!
They ran down the hill,
The pumpkins chased them,
They are chasing them still.

Jay Sharratt (9)

Past The Portal

I knew what had happened
As I stepped through that door.
My feet felt cold
And my hands fell to the floor.

I wasn't me
That I could see.
I could see the sky
But it was like waving goodbye.

The feel of the air
Beating across my heart.
A feeling too close,
Too close to part.

As I stepped through the portal,
This world is so wrong.
My future took a change,
My dystopian life.
Not too long.

Orlaith Marciniak (10)

One Last Song

One song,
To last forever,
A never-ending harmony,
To tell a tale,
Long since passed,
A story for the ages,
Told only by the sweet sound of the voices,
The voices of those,
Ancient ones,
Who would guard the prose,
Of the myths of the fae,
Of the elves,
Of knights,
Of maidens,
Of dragons,
And misjudged villains,
The story of a thousand lifetimes,
And many more.
For that,
Was what it cost.

Eve Boulter-Wang (12)

The Rush

Trinke, *drip, drip*
Join, rip, meander
Crash, fall, sprinkle
Rush, rush, rush
Expand, hush, hush

Crawl, crawl, *splash*
Rush, crash, blast
Hit bit, hit, hit
Crash, *splash*
Bang, rash, *boom*
Boom, boom
Shrink, grow

Grow, grow, grow
Grow vast wide
Still, I have lived a wonderful life
I was valiant
Here I am in the wide ocean
I am River.

Xaria Wilson (11)

Butterflies

Butterflies are creatures whose wings flutter.
Butterflies are all different colours.
Butterflies are beautiful.
Butterflies are unique.
Butterflies are so pretty, they put smiles on faces.
Butterflies are all shapes and sizes.
Butterflies are not just creatures.
Butterflies are also in your stomach.
Butterflies are making you nervous in your stomach.
Butterflies are a symbol of ADHD.
Butterflies are here to make you happy.

Darcy Bickford-Kehoe (10)

Life In The Trenches

I do not like the trenches,
And they ain't got no benches.
There is always a *boom! Boom! Boom!*
And I am doomed! Doomed! Doomed!

Whenever I peek my head out,
A machine gun goes *pow! Pow! Pow!*
And I really want to shout,
"Hey Germans, get out!"

I do not like the trenches
And they ain't got no benches.
There is always dying dying, dying
And I am not lying, lying, lying.

Alexander Dulat (10)

My Mythical Animal

With the buzzing of the bees
And the sycamore trees
A unicorn mountain appears

A rainbow spring and cupcakes fall in the rain
When you hear the unicorns sing
And the mythical bells go *ding dong ding*

In a place of fun, the unicorns run wild and free
They live in families of 3

Mum, Dad and Baby Rey don't exist
People say but I know the best
Unlike all the rest
My unicorn, Baby Rey.

Hope Davies (9)

David Bowie

D avid Robert Jones is his real name
A legendary singer, songwriter and actor
V ery accomplished musician
I man is his wife
D ebut album released in 1967

B romley was where he grew up
O therwise known as Ziggy Stardust
W orldwide record sales of over 100 million
I n 1986, he was the Goblin King in Labyrinth
E lvis shares his birthday.

James Coxshall (9)

My Tiring Day

I am face to face with nine blocks on the table.
I pull out my pocket knife,
The nine blocks stare at me.
I am ready to break them apart with my knife.
They're still staring at me...
I put my knife down on the table,
I talk myself out of it.
I look at them again -
There's one in the wrong place.
I turn it carefully...
Eventually, it's solved.
I did it!
I finally solved my Rubik's cube!
Then I go to sleep after a tiring day.

Salar Hirst (8)

You

Everybody could be pretty,
Even if you are old.
You could also be a hero,
Just don't let yourself be a mould.

Let your imagination run wild,
Not simply what you are told.
Be yourself and nobody else,
Live the magical life you behold.

Go on an adventure to where you decide,
But beware of the horrifying beast or you might die.
And whenever you are tired or frustrated,
Home is always there making you as happy as can be.

Sylvia Cheung (7)

The Best Book

A good book, it has everything,
You could learn how to cook
But this book was not an ordinary one,
It was the best book
Full of tiny trees and a big bad wolf
Even though most stories and tales are not true
I would recommend this book for you
Though you might think I am wrong
Have you seen a lizard singing a song?
You should get it, it's the best in the store
No wonder no one asks for more.

George Hill (9)

Sensational Seasons

L eaves change colours throughout the year.
E very summer the leaves help animals shelter from the fiery sun.
A utumn's red, yellow and brown leaves float down from the trees.
V eiled, winter's snow makes the leaves go.
E arly spring with blossoms sprouting like the sun rising.
S ummer's fruitful leaves grow on the beautiful trees and start another sensational season.

Isabella Wolton (8)

Imagining

I was in a building lesson,
Thinking of the holidays
Which were a blessing
I started to imagine things in my head:

I imagined that I was a knight,
Looking around, ready to fight.
I imagined a mite,
With a shark bite!

I imagined a bat
Riding a cat
With a top hat!
Then it sat on a mat

I imagined a clown
It was trying to run me down!
Then my teacher said,
"And that is how to make a shed!"

Sahil Agrawal (10)

Don't Forget!

A fairy won't mix with dairy
But a frog and a log will.

Dragons don't fit in wagons,
But a unicorn will fit in your lawn.

Elves can look at themselves,
But vampires are happier if they don't.

Leprechauns love gold,
A yeti is big a bold.

Now take all the things I've told,
Don't let it grow old...
Or it'll come out like blue cheese.

Shanellia Fernandes (11)

Dust

Dust has nowhere to go
And yet it always rushes like it does.
While it's dancing in the air
It probably has no feelings, right?
But what if it did?
Would it be thinking,
Why do these children keep blowing me?
Or *just don't crash into anything!*
Well, whatever its purpose is,
Except to give people dust mites,
Don't blow it because you will ruin its day!

Sienna Mills (10)

Dragons

D eep under the colossal volcano,
R ested a mighty dragon,
A ll around him were dazzling and exquisite jewels,
G reedily he stole all those jewels from King George,
O n the other side laid the most glamorous crown on earth,
N o one knows that the most divine thing on earth is under the volcano,
S ome dragons are lovely but this one certainly is not.

Nainika Kunisetty (11)

The Dragon's Den

A dragon tall and mighty
Rests beneath the snow
She searched the floor for dinner
While she dug her burrow

Far beneath the surface
Of the mythical meadow
The dragon sleeps in peace tonight
For her eggs began to grow

Through the winter and the spring
Dragon watched her babies glow
And every night she'd sing to them
of their adventures for tomorrow.

Bonnie Raine (10)

Strictly

S parkling sequins sparkling bright
T he dancers were ready to dance the night
R esults will determine who will win
I ntroducing the judges at the beginning of the show
C ounting the steps as they go
T rotting and prancing across the floor
L osers don't take the glitterball home
Y ikes! The scores are in, let's find out who wins.

Penelope Owen-Kubik (9)

A Solar System Far From Ours

In a huge solar system way far from ours,
There are dragons and wizards with loads of powers,
Fairies in mushrooms and magic owls in trees,
Honey that makes you extra smart from extra
smart bees,
Mice that can cook and horses as taxi drivers,
Ants as weight lifters and dolphins as divers,
It's too far away to fly in a rocket unless you
have powers
And that's what happens in the system far from ours.

Lily Caird (10)

I Want To Be...

My dream is to be successful,
And pursue the job I want.
To change the world in some way,
And be content with what happens.

I have lots of dreams,
I don't know which one.
There are loads of possibilities.
But, wow, there's a ton!

I need to work hard in school,
And figure out what I like.
I hope it will be good,
See you! It'll be a hike.

Isabel Mwangi (12)

Rainbow Sky

R unning under the rainbow beneath the bright blue sky.
A fter the leprechaun at the end of the rainbow.
I magine seeing leprechauns sitting on a pot of gold.
N ever an unhappy leprechaun.
B arter his freedom for his treasure
O nce you catch a leprechaun, you'll be granted three wishes
W ondering far and near looking under the rainbow.

Sienna Matthews-Ryan (9)

My Magic Box

I will put in my box
A pain-filled cry for help on a deserted island
A beloved book that's always just out of reach on a high-up shelf
Ignored messages from cruel horrid bullies.

I will put in my box
Spreading hope and winning just to be destroyed
A beloved faded memory of childhood in black and white
A long-lost sibling finally reunited with her loving sister.

Issy Heron (9)

The Sound Of Nature

Rose petals danced from the cavern above,
Sunlight gaping in,
A thousand cantering horses marching to the beat of a drum.

An olive tree grew by the river,
Green fruits entwined around its branches.
A feverish golden glimmer in one's eye,
Enough to drown a city.

Magenta lilies sprung from green pastures,
While lambs grazed in avocado fields.

The sound of nature.

Zea Windett (12)

The River

Whenever you hear the trickling sound,
Whenever you see the beautiful blue creature,
Whenever the river bends around,
Whenever you see the lovely, green nature,
Late in the night when everyone is asleep with
closed mouths,
Why does it have its mouth open towards the south,

Whenever the trees are swaying,
The rivers are singing,
You can hear the loud noise,
Sometimes, you'll shout aloud.

Vihanishree Karthik (10)

All Things Football

I am a footy fan
I love to play football whenever I can
All the little things about it too
From football cards to brand-new shoes

Opponent smashing
Feet thrashing
Card trading
Rain lashing

Team meeting
Goals repeating
Shoe booting
Healthy eating

Great skilling
Space filling
Record slaying
Footie playing.

Gruffydd Mundy (8)

Cats

I like cats

L ove them in fact
O nly Dad won't let me have one
V irtually every day, I think about them non-stop
E ven when I do all his chores he still won't let me

C ats are joyful and fun
A nd they make me smile
T hey could even become my best friend
S o please can I get one, Dad?

Aaliyah Girach (8)

The Perfect Spell

Magic round each corner
The perfect spell is close
If you don't get away soon
You will be a goner

Don't look far
There is no need
It is in the past

One more time
And you will be in its mighty grasp
The wolfasauras is its name
Its powers are second to none.
I would tell you but it's past my bedtime.
So good night.

Layla Saunders (10)

The Friendly Tree

It moves with the wind like a kite in the sky
And it has green leaves as its sign
It blooms with flowers as a gentle fragrance
And it is home for many animals and birds
It has roots deep in the soil
And it has medicinal properties upon boil
It shows its branches up in the sky
And it bears the fruit which people buy
So those are friendly trees all around us.

Manha Siriyala (9)

The Glory Of The Game

Messi is the GOAT
Don't worry, he has been on a boat

When the game starts to flow
Listen for the ref as he might blow

Red card, yellow card - get off the pitch
The fans call the referee a rotten witch

Running for that ball
Suddenly a big fall

Handshakes and high-fives with your friend
The glorious game comes to an end.

Darcy Keenan (10)

Mysterious Friends

Dogs, cats, bats and spiders
But none of them are writers

The dog tried to walk on the log
We saw him in the fog

The cat went to town
And acted like a clown

The spiders made a run
It all looked like fun.

The bat flew out of the cave
And hit a big wave

These are the animals
That are personally my fave.

Willow Keenan (8)

Fly, Little Sparrow

Fly, little sparrow, and spread your wings,
Open up and take dear flight.

Sing, little sparrow, and let your voice ring,
Open your beak and sing what is right.

Rule, little sparrow, for you are King,
Command your people with all your might.

Come, little sparrow for your presence sings,
Journey, little sparrow - far into the night.

Mathilde Lacey (12)

One Ella

Only one of me,
And no one can get a better one.
No one plays football like me,
No one reads books like me.
No one, there is no one like me at all.
I am me, I am I, you aren't my,
You aren't I, you aren't me!
No one can cry my tears;
No one can cough my coughs.
No one sees what I see,
No one I say; no one is like me.

Ella Campbell (10)

Christmas Has Started

C hristmas is finally coming
H ave you seen the spectacular sight?
R inging bells are humming melodies
I cannot ignore it
S plendid choirs sing beautifully
T winkling lights glow peacefully
M ince pies crispy, delicious and hot
A tasty cup of nice hot chocolate
S anta is coming.

Ayona Sarkar (10)

Cherry Leaves

The cherry leaves thrive
As they dance on the vines

Luscious long grass
Have lots of flowers to pass
People pick them and put them in a vase

Cherry leaves fly through the heavenly skies
I can see it through my bright blue eyes

As the birds fly through the horizontal sky
They flap their wings and chirp goodbye.

Vanesa Bareisyte (9)

Never Grow Up

I was told to never grow up,
But still, I am here grown up,
I tried to stop it, I did,
But I couldn't,
I got taller and taller,
The birthdays came and went,
I couldn't stop the growth,
I loved the little me,
But I am already twenty-three...
I don't want to write any more,
Because soon I will be twenty-four.

Elsie Tatnall (9)

Universe Of Wonders

Universe of wonders,
Anything you want it to be,
Star-spangled skies,
Dragons with glittering eyes,
Temples of gold,
Amazing stories being told,
Mountains of snow,
Fascinating things people know,
It's a universe of wonders,
So make it your own,
One thing is for sure,
You'll never want to go home!

Amelie Sanchez-Phillips (10)

Flowers

Flowers blossom in the middle of the spring
Somehow it triggers the birds to sing
Flowers are beautiful like you and me
Take a closer look and you will see
Little honeybees coming out of the flowers
Flowers grow more during showers
Here's a little fact before we leave
Flowers aren't so different to humongous trees.

Indigo Emery (9)

Have You Ever Seen A Movie?

I haven't even got a job yet and it's gone,
It takes from the darkest web,
Not even Google is safe.

What's real?
What's not?
It steals from others and takes as its own.
Not a credit in their name.

No ethics,
No morals,
Do you know what's beneath the surface?
So I must ask,
Have you ever seen a movie? How does it end?

Summer Jones-Loizou (12)

The Five Children

Children were playing a game
As they played they saw a creature
"That doesn't belong there," shouted Lilly
It had a long horn, eyes and a thick furry face
The teeth were smelly
Its arms and legs were like a monkey
Bella said, "Can we take it home?"
Everybody said, "No!"

Steffina Caroline (8)

Bamboo Forest

At sunrise, the elderly monk sighs,
A serene stream flows by.
Animals there, like bears, arrive in pairs.
There are still mischievous macaques and bolting bats.
There are still passionate pandas and slippery salamanders.
All living in the forest, they call home,
All roaming cheerfully in this luscious dome.

Ori Sivayokan (10)

Seahorse

S trange stripes on zebra seahorses
E legant body
A mazing camouflage to hide from predators
H over upright in the shimmering water
O n the seaweed beds, they swim
R oaring waves splash above them
S uper slow they move
E very seahorse has delicate fins.

Oliver Wells (8)

Animals Together

A flock of birds to feast your eyes
N avigating through the gorgeous sky
I ntelligent reptiles slithering around
M ammals here and all around
A nimals squeaking with different sounds
L ike lots of elephants all around
S loths are so slow they don't even know.

Chloe Marshall (8)

Kingfisher

Bright blue kingfisher
Swooping low over trickling streams
Perching peacefully on smooth branches
Flashes of blue left, right and centre
Diving into roaring rivers for fleeing fish
A flurry of feathers, then up soars the kingfisher
Victorious as ever soaring up with its prize
This is the kingfisher.

Eleanor Newbold (9)

Fire

The flames danced around the ring of stones,
Condemned to life imprisonment.
They rocketed up to the sky.
The smoke spiralled upwards into greying clouds.
Time passed and the fire grew ever weaker,
Glowing and glittering in the embers
Waiting to be released.
A thousand stars in the ashy darkness.

Grace Harding (12)

The Snacks

One October 31st (Halloween) the candy came to life
They went on a mission to build the biggest chocolate bar ever
After 10 days, they got all together from all the 7 continents
Asia, Africa, North America, South America, Antarctica, Europe and Australasia
And they built the most enormous chocolate bar ever.

Franek Buksa (10)

Winter

W ind whispering through the snowy winter
I cy lakes being frozen, someone to skate
N umbing of hands and feet in the absence of boots and gloves
T emperature cools down even below zero
E veryone is happy when it is snowy
R unning and running, the snow is falling.

Athmika Jeyakanth (10)

Emotions

Sadness is just a feeling
Happiness is just a word
Anger is just rage
Disgust is just nasty
They will never be able to feel them
They are just words
Words will always make you
Think you feel them,
But you don't
So what is the reason for them
If you don't need them?

Sophie Shooter (12)

Magical Day

One day, a sunny day
Something came out
It was a cricket stadium
They built for a year
I went inside
There was no grass at all
I thought, *what is this place?*
Is it a house?
Is it a stadium?
Is it space?
Who knows?

Aarush Vijay Bhaskar (7)

Snowy Month

There is a patch of white shiny snow.
The snow is so amazing.
In winter it is so calming.
Children love the snow.
The snow is so glittery.
The snow is so satisfying.
The snow is so fun
Because you can make snowmen.
Inside my house, it is so cosy and warm.

Mirsada Gjoni (8)

I See...

A ll over the world, I see...

J aguars that are spotty
U mbrellas held by orangutans
N ice sloths crawling along a tree
G iraffes eating grass
L eopards playing on the ground
E lephants spraying water on my face.

Dylan May (8)

Pandas

P andas running, running far
A raging fire is behind them
N othing is left from the destruction of the fire
D angerous fire continued to follow them
A s soon as they left the forest the fire stopped and
they were...
S afe again!

Edward Wells (9)

The Twin Guards

Two twin guards who stand by the icy gate,
Anyone who approaches has sealed their fate,
With a swing of a sword,
And a meeting with the board,
Anyone who approaches has sealed their fate,
Because no one lives to tell the tale
Of what lies beyond the icy gate.

Nia MacKean (12)

I Am Me

I want to be a farmer
I want to write
I want to be a businesswoman
Because I have the right
I want to make stories
I want to take care of animals
I can do anything that I want
I have confidence
I believe
I can do anything
I can be me.

Hope Miles (9)

Medusa

M edusa is a character from Greek mythology. She had
E yes that turned onlookers into stone
D aughter of two sea gods.
U nlike other creatures, she was mortal.
S erpents' hair.
A thena cursed Medusa to have a cold stare.

Micky Murray Slater (11)

A Forest

A beautiful sunny morning

F un for a football match
O n a beautiful sunny morning
R un to get on time
E njoy the beautiful weather
S unny like the stars
T ry to be on time for a sunny football match.

Laurynas Lipski (9)

Magical Pixie Land

Their dust gives you wings
As the treasure gives you things
Nothing is ever better than...
Pixie Land
Home of the true fairies

Love will share as your hair develops
Into pink perfect pixie dust
There is no such thing as browny rust.

Hafsa Nasir Choudhry (11)

I Love, I Cherish

I love my cat, her emerald eyes
Give me a cold shiver
When she catwalks by
I cherish my Calico
She has been my whole life
Love isn't just about pictures
It's about every moment
You hold onto in your heart
Her name is Queenie.

Connie-Ann Marsh (8)

Taylor Swift

T he Tortured Poets Department
A ll Too Well
Y ellow
L over
O ut Of The World
R ed

S peak Now
W ow!
I Knew You Were Trouble
F olklore
T aylor Swift.

Joseph Delannoy (9)

Earth Vs Meteor

A meteor is coming
S top the meteor
T errified people everywhere
"E veryone run!" says the mayor
R unning people here and there
O h no, it's speeding up
I have an idea
D ig!

Leo Carter-Garrick (7)

Fabulous Food

"What's for tea?" I ask Mummy
Chicken nuggets, oh so yummy

Crispy on the outside, soft on the inside
They are the best food I have ever tried

I love to shove them in my belly
Then ask what's for pudding... jelly!

Emily Skitt (6)

My Brain

Sad, angry, happy, silly
I feel confused about what they are doing
Yellow, red, black, confusing
A big scrambled mess
A deep breath, count to ten
Time out, feeling calm
Relaxed, happy, peaceful
Feels like a calm wave in the sea.

Alex Goodey (8)

Halloween

The wind in the trees
The excitement in the breeze
Children with buckets of treats
Decorations, pumpkins and lights
For this only happens once of all the nights
Soon everyone is sleeping
And the great pumpkin is carefully creeping.

Violet Kurn (9)

Stories Can

Stories can be big
Stories can be small
Stories can make you fall off your stool
Stories can be true or not
Stories can be about guns filled with snot
Stories can be about little girls who moan
But all stories bring you back home.

Rosa Burns-Newton (8)

Sports

Haiku poetry

Sporting achievements
Go amazing Great Britain
The Olympic sports

2024
Are held in Paris this year
Busy in Paris

Who will win this year?
Let's go, it's game time right now
Sports are amazing.

Esme Buckley (9)

Health

Health keeps you alive,
So give it a high five!
Give your allergy medication
Have no fear, it's just an infection.

Just a plaster, off you go
No more blood will ever show.
First aid kit,

You are very fit!

Kinga Dionisjew (8)

The Seasons Grow

S easons come and seasons go
E njoy the seasons as they grow
A s the leaves begin to fall
S eeds move in and start to sow
O nly one thing we need to know
N o rain, no water, no plants will grow.

Callum Marshall (8)

Spider Cider

Rotten rat tails
A dash of dark diesel
A strike of enemy's underwear
So beware!
A spray of salty seawater
A dollop of dark demon blood
A slimy sardine
And a blood-red beetle!

Ariana Parker (8)

Quails!

Big quails, small quails,
Eat and sleep.
Small quails squeak,
And big quails chirp.

Calm chicks, jumpy chicks,
Play and flop.
Calm chicks waddle,
And jumpy chicks hop.

Shun Hey Lee (9)

Snake Vs The Ladder

There once was a snake with a ladder
Who said, "I am more radder!"
But the ladder disagreed
And said, "I shall win against te!"
Then the snake was beaten by the ladder.

Janvi Chalasani (11)

Otter

O tters like to play all day
T hey love it if they're all okay
T hey eat all kinds of food
E ating is their favourite thing
R oaming the rivers all day.

Sophie Newbold (7)

Ambitious Aphrodite

A dventurous
P assionate
H onourable
R ose
O bservant
D oves
I rreplaceable
T reasure
E legant.

Cleo Johnson-Duncombe (10)

Try And Guess My Animal!

I can swim,
I'm always hungry,
I've got inky-black eyes,
And a large snout to sniff,
My fins are enormous,
What am I?

Answer: A shark.

Neo Montaque (8)

Flowers

In the garden, flowers bloom,
Petals bright, dispelling gloom.
In the sun they rise and glow,
Sharing beauty as they grow.

Sophia Serene

Crows

A haiku

Big black or white bird
Annual and diurnal crows
Caw! Caw! The crow's screech.

Victoria Anyaegbu (10)

Daffodil

A haiku

Dancing in the breeze
Petals flutter in the wind
Beautiful flowers.

Caden Hamlyn-Harris (11)

Musca Domestica

A haiku

Very, very black
Very pesky, annoying
Get off my pasta!

Ochre Chidley (8)

YOUNG WRITERS INFORMATION

We hope you have enjoyed reading this book – and that you will continue to in the coming years.

If you're the parent or family member of an enthusiastic poet or story writer, do visit our website **www.youngwriters.co.uk/subscribe** and sign up to receive news, competitions, writing challenges and tips, activities and much, much more! There's lots to keep budding writers motivated!

If you would like to order further copies of this book, or any of our other titles, then please give us a call or order via your online account.

Young Writers
Remus House
Coltsfoot Drive
Peterborough
PE2 9BF
(01733) 890066
info@youngwriters.co.uk

Join in the conversation!
Tips, news, giveaways and much more!

YoungWritersUK   YoungWritersCW

youngwriterscw   youngwriterscw